W9-BPN-100

TALES
MUMMIES
TELL

PATRICIA LAUBER
TALES MUMMIES TELL

HarperCollins*Publishers*

Acknowledgments

While general information about mummies appears in many sources, in writing this book I have drawn heavily on the work of a handful of scientists who, with their colleagues, have made major contributions to the field in recent years and written engagingly of their discoveries. In particular, I should like to acknowledge my debt to: Dr. James E. Harris, who x-rayed the pharaohs; Dr. Rosalie David, who led the Manchester team in examining mummy No. 1770; Dr. Marvin Allison, who studied the mummies of Peru; and Dr. P. V. Glob, whose account of the finding of the Tollund and Grauballe men, along with other bog bodies, remains the primary source for anyone who writes on this subject.

I am also grateful for the assistance of scientists and staff members at the National Museum in Copenhagen, the Museum of Prehistory at Aarhus, and the Silkeborg Museum.

Last, but not least, I should like to thank Bette Birnbaum, who handled the long and complex job of photo research with skill, perseverance, and unflagging enthusiasm.

Library of Congress Cataloging-in-Publication Data
Lauber, Patricia.
  Tales mummies tell.

  Summary: Explains how the study of mummies,
both natural and man-made, including a frozen baby
mammoth found in Siberia and the human mummies
of Egypt, Peru, and Denmark, can reveal information
about ancient civilizations and prehistoric life.
  1. Mummies—Juvenile literature. [1. Mummies.
2. Civilization—History] I. Title.
GT3340.L38   1985   930.1′028′5   83-46172
ISBN 0-690-04388-0
ISBN 0-690-04389-9 (lib. bdg.)

Designed by Al Cetta

For Sally,
who suggested it

Contents

TALES
MUMMIES
TELL

*Woolly mammoths,
shown in this painting,
disappeared at the end
of the last ice age.*

1. A Mammoth Mummy

One long-ago summer's day, a baby woolly mammoth some-how lost his mother. He was no more than seven or eight months old, so young that he had only milk teeth and still depended on his mother for food. As he wandered around his home range, near the Arctic Circle, his body fat was quickly used up. Frantic with hunger, he tried to eat dirt and plants. Then he had an accident and fell, perhaps into an icy pit, where he soon died. In the far north, summer is short. The body froze and became encased in ice. Cave-ins buried it under six feet of earth. The ground froze and stayed frozen, except for the top few inches, which thawed each summer. In this natural deep freeze, the body of the baby mammoth was preserved for thousands of years. It became a mummy, which is the term now used for any well-preserved body, whether animal or human.

The mummy was found in June 1977. At that time Soviet gold prospectors were working near a stream in northeastern Siberia. One was running a bulldozer, digging out mud and frozen ground, when he struck a big block of muddy ice with something dark inside. Curious about what he had found, the prospector changed the flow of the stream and used its water to melt some of the ice. In a short time, the shape of a baby mammoth appeared.

The discovery was of great interest to Soviet scientists who study mammoths. Woolly mammoths, which were relatives of today's elephants, managed to survive a long period of drastic changes in the earth's climate. They lived through times when heavy snows fell, when great glaciers formed and grew so big that mile-thick sheets of ice swallowed huge areas of land for thousands of years. They lived through times when the air warmed and the glaciers shrank, releasing floods of meltwater. Yet when the glaciers last melted and drew back, about 9,000 to 12,000 years ago, the woolly mammoths died out. How and why they did remains a mystery.

We know about mammoths from the cave drawings of Stone Age peoples and from the remains of mammoths that have been found. Over the years countless bones and tusks have been found in the far north. From time to time parts of woolly mammoths have been discovered in the frozen ground, but whole mammoths are rare. The few discovered in the 1800s rotted away or were eaten by animals before scientists could study them. The ones found in this century have not been complete. The Soviet prospectors' find, which they named Dima, was the first whole mammoth mummy that modern scientists had ever had a chance to study. In addition, only once before, in Alaska, had anyone found remains of a baby mammoth.

The mummy was flown to a laboratory in the north, where it was refrigerated to keep it from rotting. Later it was flown to Leningrad for detailed study. Samples of material from the body were shared with scientists in the United States who were trying to find out, among other things, the exact relationship of mammoths and elephants.

Early studies showed that Dima was about 4 feet tall and 4 feet long and weighed 198 pounds. His trunk measured 22 inches and had two "fingers" at the end, just like the ones that can be seen in cave paintings. The hide was now separated from the body, but in life Dima had had a shaggy, chestnut-colored coat. The soft, thick undercoat was 3 to 4 inches long and protected by a covering of wiry hairs up to 10 inches long. The trunk was furry and the outer ears were tiny. Like all woolly mammoths, Dima was well equipped to live in the far north, with a covering that trapped and held in body heat. By contrast, today's elephants live in warm or hot climates and are equipped to get rid of body heat. They have no fur, only bristles, on their leathery hides. Their huge outer ears provide extra surface area from which heat can escape.

It was clear that Dima had been hungry: His ribs stuck out through his skin. The stomach and other intestines provided

Except around the feet, Dima's shaggy coat was separated from the body.

more clues to what had happened. In them was only a trace of his mother's milk. Alone, he had eaten mostly dirt. With just three milk teeth, he had not been able to chew plant food but had simply swallowed some roots, stems, grass, and grass seeds. The presence of grass seeds showed that Dima had died in summer, the time of year when these seeds form. The month was most likely August, which is late summer in the arctic.

The excellent condition of the mummy was the chief clue to the kind of place in which Dima died. It must have been a cold one, cold enough to keep the body from decaying before it froze. And because the body was buried, it must have been a place where cave-ins or landslides could occur, such as a pit or the bank of a stream.

To find the age of the mummy, scientists made use of a built-in atomic clock. This is how the clock works:

Certain kinds of atoms are radioactive—they keep breaking down by giving off tiny parts of themselves. Among these atoms are those of carbon 14, which is a radioactive variety of carbon. Carbon 14 forms when the atmosphere is bombarded by cosmic rays. When it combines with oxygen, it forms carbon dioxide. This radioactive carbon dioxide mixes with the other carbon dioxide in the air.

Plants take in carbon dioxide, which they use to make their food. And so they also take in carbon 14. Every bit of a living plant contains a tiny amount of carbon 14. Animals feed on

Sketch shows how Dima may have died,
by falling into an ice shaft.

plants or on other animals that eat plants. As a result, every animal's body also contains a tiny amount of carbon 14. The carbon 14 keeps breaking down, but new supplies are continually being added.

When an animal or a plant dies, it stops taking in carbon 14. No new supplies are added, but the carbon 14 already in the tissues continues to break down. It does so at a fixed and steady rate, which is described by its half-life—the time required for half its atoms to break down.

Carbon 14 has a half-life of about 5,600 years. This means that some 5,600 years after a plant or animal dies, half the carbon 14 atoms present at the time of death are left; the rest have broken down into a different kind of atom. After another 5,600 years have passed, half of the half—a quarter—are left. After another 5,600 years, an eighth of the carbon 14 atoms are left, and so on. After some 50,000 years there is almost no carbon 14 left, although scientists can still use that tiny bit.

Because carbon 14 breaks down at this steady rate, scientists can use it to date once-living things, such as Dima, that are up to 100,000 years old. They can analyze a sample of tissue and find out how much carbon 14 is in it. They compare this result with the amount of carbon 14 in an equal amount of living tissue. They can then calculate how long ago the plant or animal died. In the same way, if you had a clock that would run 24 hours without winding and someone told you the clock had 3 hours left to run, you would know it had been running for 21 hours.

Using one method of carbon-14 dating, Soviet scientists found that Dima's mummy was 40,000 years old. American scientists, using a different method, found the atomic clock had been running for 27,000 years. Either date makes Dima one of the oldest mummies in the world.

The studies of Dima did not solve the mystery of why woolly mammoths died out, but the mummy did tell of a brief life in a world that vanished long ago. And that is one of the chief reasons why scientists study the many kinds of mummies that have been found. Some give glimpses of single lives. Others tell much about worlds that we have never known.

Although the most famous,
Egyptian mummies,
such as this well-wrapped
one with its coffin,
are far from being
the only mummies.

2. Many Kinds of Mummies

The word *mummies* usually makes people think of ancient Egyptians wrapped in bands of linen. Egyptian mummies are the most famous, but they are far from being the only ones. Peoples in many parts of the world have made mummies of their dead, and a great many other mummies have formed naturally, as Dima's did.

Most mummies, whether natural or manmade, formed by rapid drying. Ordinarily, when a living thing dies, decay soon sets in. The decay is caused by bacteria, molds, and other small forms of life. As they feed on dead material, they break it down. The material, which is rich in minerals that plants need, is added to the soil. In this way the material is recycled. It is used by plants, which are eaten by animals. To do their work, bacteria and other small living things need water. They cannot multiply or grow without it. If dead material dries out rapidly and stays dry, decay does not take place. In fact, for thousands of years people have been preserving meat and fish this way, by drying them in the sun or packing them in salt, which draws water from the tissues.

Mummies have often formed naturally in deserts, where hot dry sands rapidly drew water out of the body tissues. Probably the first Egyptian mummies were made by accident in this way, when early settlers of the Nile Valley buried their dead in the desert, outside the fertile farmland.

Others have formed in similar ways. Copper Man is a South American mummy that formed naturally with the help of dry air and salts. This mummy was once a copper miner who lived and worked around A.D. 800 in the Atacama Desert of northern Chile. He was in a mine, hammering rock and prying out copper ore, when the tunnel in which he was working collapsed and killed him. His mummy was found in 1899, with its arms still out in a working position. His hair was neatly braided and he wore a loincloth. Near him were the tools of his trade: four coiled baskets for hauling out rock; a rawhide bag for ore; a stone hammer; a spade-shaped stone tool. He was named Copper Man because the copper salts that helped preserve his body combined with oxygen and stained his body a dull green.

In some parts of the world, bodies placed in certain caves have air dried rapidly and turned into mummies. In Palermo, Sicily, there is an underground burial cave called the Capuchin Catacombs. Its walls are lined with some 8,000 mummies of men, women, and children who died in the 1800s. All

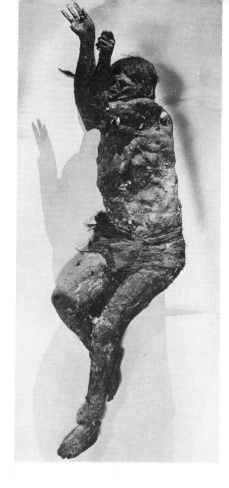

After its discovery, the mummy of Copper Man was bought and sold several times and exhibited in Chile and the United States. The mummy early lost a little finger and a little toe to souvenir hunters.

are dressed in their best clothes, their bodies preserved by the dryness of the air.

Indian mummies have been found in the caves of Kentucky. One, for example, was discovered lying on a ledge in Salts Cave in 1875. Apparently the salts of the cave had absorbed moisture from the air and the movement of dry air had mummified the body. Named Little Alice, the mummy was exhibited for many years before being taken to the University of Kentucky in 1958. There careful examination showed that Little Alice was actually a boy who had died at

After being exhibited for many years, Little Alice was found to be a boy—and renamed Little Al.

the age of nine or ten. Carbon-14 dating gave an age for the mummy, now known as Little Al, of about 2,000 years.

The dry climate of the American Southwest, especially of Arizona, produced a number of well-preserved Indian mummies. Some of the earliest belonged to the Basket Makers, a group of wanderers who lived in caves and rock shelters of the region between A.D. 100 and 700. These mummies seem to have been made on purpose, to have been placed in caves so that the bodies would be preserved. With the mummies were various goods—sandals, beads, baskets, weapons, pipes. These may mean that the Basket Makers believed in a life after death and were providing the dead with what they might need. So far no one knows. Nor does anyone yet know

This young male Basket Maker
died about A.D. 300 to 500
and was mummified
in the Canyon del Muerto.

why only some persons were chosen to become cave mummies—among them infants, children, women, and men—when most of the dead were buried in pits.

Rapid freezing created the mummies of Dima and many other animals. It has also produced human mummies.

In 1972, for example, the frozen body of an elderly Eskimo woman washed out of a cliff along the shore of Saint Lawrence Island in the Bering Sea. Scientists who studied the mummy found that the woman had died around A.D. 400, when an earthquake or a landslide destroyed her house. Buried in the ruins, under a deep covering of earth, the body froze and was preserved for some 1,600 years. It was so well preserved that the scientists could study the tattooing on the

[13]

woman's hands and arms and also identify the diseases from which she had suffered.

Soviet scientists have found the frozen remains of ancient nomads known as Scythians, high in the Altai Mountains on the border between Siberia and Outer Mongolia. Between 2,000 and 3,000 years ago, Scythian tribes wandered the treeless plains of Eurasia from the Black Sea to China. They were horsemen and herdsmen who raided Greek and Persian outposts when they could and traded when they couldn't.

Much of what is known about the Scythians comes from the writings of Herodotus, a famous historian of ancient Greece. He described, among other things, the ceremonies that took place when a Scythian king died and the way his

Scythian horseman is one of the figures used to decorate a large piece of felt cloth found in a frozen burial chamber. His clothing is like that found in tombs. Scythian men wore long narrow trousers made of soft leather, felt stockings, high boots with soft soles, and capelike tunics. Women also wore tunics and felt stockings. Their dress boots were made of leopard fur and decorated with beads on the soles, which may mean that they had a habit of sitting cross-legged so that the patterned soles showed.

Horses, like the one shown, had their manes cropped and their tails bobbed, with the long hairs braided. A saddle was made of two pillows stuffed with grass or deer hair and sewn together. Saddles and saddle cloths were decorated with felt cutouts of wild animals. The mummified horses wore slipcovers on their heads. One had two large antlers attached to the top and a fur outline of a tiger on the muzzle.

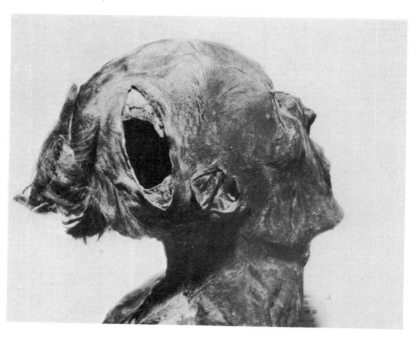

In embalming a body, the Scythians removed the brain through a hole chiseled in the skull.

body was embalmed, or preserved. More information has come from the tombs and mummies themselves.

To embalm the body of a king, the Scythians removed the parts most likely to decay: the stomach, intestines, and other internal organs. A hole was chiseled in the skull and the brain taken out. The insides of the arms and legs were slit, and sometimes muscles were removed. A preservative, perhaps salt, may have been used inside the body. Once the arms and legs were padded with grass or horsehair, the body was sewn up. Finally, the king's body was covered with wax, placed on a wagon, and carried about for 40 days to all the different tribes.

When a tribe received the corpse, all the men cropped their hair short. Each also cut off a piece of his ear, made a cut around his arm, and thrust an arrow through his left hand. The journey ended with the most distant tribe, where a large square grave, about 15 feet deep, had been prepared. The body was laid in the grave, which was then covered with beams and thatching. The Scythians killed and buried with the king one of his wives, his personal servants, and some of his horses. They also placed in the grave the finest of the king's possessions and some gold cups. At the end they

Scythian chiefs and nobles, such as this cavalry leader, were also embalmed before burial. Horses were killed at the time of the funeral ceremonies and buried with their owners.

raised a huge mound of boulders and earth above the tomb.

Embalming preserved the bodies for a time, but it was cold air that turned them into mummies. The layer of boulders covering a grave was not airtight, and so the grave filled with frigid air during the mountain winter. Because cold air is heavier than warm air, it tends to sink, while warm air tends to rise. As a result, the graves stayed icy cold even during the short summer. In these natural refrigerators, the bodies of the Scythians, together with their clothing and their horses, were preserved. Despite the plundering of grave robbers, enough remains to bring to life the art and skills of an almost forgotten people.

The hot, wet climate of a jungle does not seem a likely place for mummies, but the Jivaro Indians, who live in the High Amazon River basin of Ecuador and Peru, have mastered a special kind of mummy making. The Jivaros are headhunters who preserve and shrink the heads of slain enemies.

Head-hunting is a very old form of primitive warfare that has been practiced in many parts of the world. In general, when a warrior took a head, he believed that he was taking certain qualities of the victim, such as strength, courage, or wisdom. These qualities were then added to his own or to those of his tribe.

Some headhunters mummified the heads of their enemies by drying or smoking them, but the Jivaros have specialized in making shrunken heads, which are called *tsantsas*. They shrink the head to the size of a fist but manage to keep the original features of the face.

Because hair does not shrink, that of a tsantsa is long and full.

Making a tsantsa is a serious business. Almost every step is accompanied by a religious ceremony. It also calls for a lot of skillful work.

The warrior first cuts off the head as close to the trunk of the body as possible, keeping the skin of the neck. He makes a cut along the scalp from front to back and peels the scalp away from the skull so that the two halves hang outward, like sacks. The next step is the hardest, and the headhunter may be helped by a fellow tribesman with more experience. Using a sharp tool made of bamboo, shell, or flint, he separates the skin from the bones of the face, taking great care not to damage the nose, lips, eyelids, and ears.

Removal of the bones causes the skin of the head to shrink to half its original size. To shrink it still more and keep it from decaying, the head is soaked for several days in a kind of broth made from boiled plants. Later the openings of the eyes and mouth are sewed closed to keep evil spirits from escaping through them. The scalp is also sewed up. The only opening left is at the base of the neck. Into it the Jivaro pours hot sand that has been heated in a special piece of pottery. The heat causes the head to shrink still more. As it shrinks, the headhunter keeps modeling the features. Oils are applied to the skin. Because hair does not shrink, that of the tsantsa is extremely long and full. It may be braided and decorated with beads or feathers. When the tsantsa is finished, there is a big celebration for the whole tribe.

There is still another way that mummies have formed, whether by accident or on purpose. Bodies have been pre-

When searchers located his coffin and opened it, they were startled to find themselves looking at the mummy of John Paul Jones.

served in various liquids that kill bacteria or greatly slow their action. One of these was the body of John Paul Jones, naval hero of the Revolutionary War.

Jones died in Paris, France, on July 18, 1792 at the age of 45. He was buried and forgotten until an American ambassador to France began a search for his grave. In 1905 the searchers thought they had found the right coffin and opened it to make sure. They were startled to find themselves staring at the mummy of John Paul Jones. Apparently, his friends had intended to preserve the body and ship it to the United States. So they had placed it in a lead coffin filled with alcohol. The body was so well preserved that anyone familiar with the portraits of Jones could tell whose body this was. It was so well preserved that doctors who performed an autopsy could tell that although he had been suffering from jaundice and kidney disease, the cause of death had been pneumonia. The body was returned to the United States for a hero's burial.

Perhaps the best-preserved mummy known is that of a Chinese lady who died some 2,100 years ago in the province of Hunan. Her body was preserved in a slightly acid fluid that contained a form of mercury, then sealed in an airtight coffin. Exactly who she was is not certain, but it is clear that she was a person of high rank. It is equally clear that those who buried her followed ancient teachings and paid honor to her family, both living and dead. They believed that her life after death depended on how well they observed funeral customs and how well they preserved her body.

Their efforts came to light in the early 1970s, when the Chinese government was building a new hospital. An ancient, 65-foot-high burial mound lay in the way. The government decided to excavate it.

Workers dug through the mound for four months before they came to its bottom. Whatever lay within the tomb itself was sealed inside a thick layer of white clay. Beneath the clay was five tons of charcoal, meant to soak up any water that seeped through the clay. Under the charcoal was a series of beautifully decorated coffins, one within another.

Prying open the heavy outer coffins, scientists found paintings, silks, musical instruments, small wooden statues. All were from the early part of the Western Han Dynasty, which ruled China from 206 B.C. to A.D. 24. All were made from materials that normally decay with the passing of time. But because air and water had been sealed out, all were perfectly preserved.

The sixth and innermost coffin held a wonderfully preserved mummy of a woman wrapped in silk. Most mummies have dry, leathery skin. This mummy had flesh that was still elastic. Its joints could be bent. The dark hair was still well anchored in the scalp.

Chinese medical scientists were curious to know more about a person who lived 2,100 years ago, and so they performed an autopsy. They found that the lady had been about 50 years old and somewhat overweight at the time of her death. She had lost half her teeth, and some of the remaining ones were badly worn. Although the brain had collapsed into a shapeless mass, all the internal organs were well preserved. The stomach held 138 muskmelon seeds, which she must have eaten shortly before her death.

The cause of death was apparently a heart attack. The lady had suffered from hardening of the arteries, which is caused by a buildup of hard material called plaque on the inside of arteries. The arteries leading to her heart were nearly blocked. She had also suffered from gallstones, tuberculosis, and worms. A bony growth on her spine must have caused

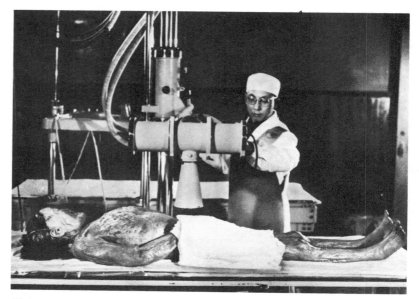

Chinese doctor x-rays the mummy of a woman who was first thought to be Lady Li, wife of the marquis of Tai. Later it was suggested that she was of even higher rank, but just who she really was is not clear.

severe back and leg pains, which is probably why paintings of the lady show her walking with a cane.

The doctors guessed that her death had been sudden. If she had been ill for a long time and bedridden, she would probably have developed bedsores—and there were none.

Learning about the health of ancient peoples is another major reason why scientists study mummies. From such studies they hope one day to learn where various diseases came from in the first place. They hope to trace diseases and learn whether they have changed—and if so, how. They found the autopsy of the Chinese lady interesting because it showed that 2,100 years ago she suffered from diseases that are well known today. Her tomb also told something about religious beliefs, funeral customs, and art during the Western Han Dynasty. In the same way, the many, many mummies of Egypt offer a chance to learn about the beliefs, customs, and health of a large and ancient group of people.

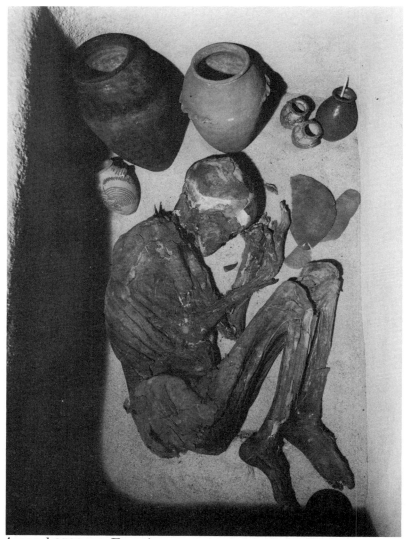

Around 3500 B.C. Egyptians were buried in shallow graves where sun-heated sand rapidly dried out the bodies. As this reconstructed grave shows, a dead person was placed in a sleeping position and supplied with objects needed to continue everyday life.

3. Mummy Making in Egypt

The ancient Egyptians believed in a life after death. They also believed that the body had to be preserved if a dead person was to have a happy afterlife. The beliefs were old ones. They can be traced back some 6,000 or 7,000 years to the early people who farmed the Nile Valley and buried their dead in graves scooped out of the hot, dry desert sands. Each body was carefully placed in its grave and accompanied by simple grave goods—pottery, fishhooks, knife blades, beads, ivory combs, hairpins. All were things the person had used in life. All suggest hope for an afterlife very much like daily life in the Nile Valley. Usually a small mound was built over a grave, but it was never large enough to interfere with the warming effect of the sun. The bodies became natural mummies made on purpose. Some were so well preserved that the features of their faces are still clear today.

As hundreds of years passed, civilization advanced and Egypt became a united country that was ruled by a pharaoh. Among the many changes that took place were ones in burial customs. The body of an ordinary person was now laid out in a wooden coffin, which was placed in a burial pit topped by a wooden roof. The tombs of pharaohs and nobles were much more elaborate. They included underground rooms for ceremonies and for grave goods and the bodies of servants who would serve their masters in the afterlife. The rooms were roofed over and covered above ground by large structures made of mud bricks, which were probably imitations of palaces or fortresses.

The changes created a problem. Before burial, bodies were carefully wrapped in strips of linen. But while the bandaging preserved the shape of the body, it did not preserve the body itself. Neither did the tomb, which separated the body from the drying effect of the desert sand. In addition, the dampness of the tomb encouraged bacteria and decay.

The decay forced the ancient Egyptians to search for ways to treat bodies so that they would be preserved in their tombs. Exactly what they did in the beginning is not clear, because their efforts were not very successful. Archeologists have found parts of bodies, such as the bones of an arm wrapped in linen and decorated with jewelry. But these remains give no clue as to how the bodies were treated.

The first evidence of experiments with making mummies comes from around 2600 B.C., in a period known as the Old Kingdom. It shows that the embalmers, who prepared bodies for burial, had taken two giant steps forward. They had learned to remove from a body the parts that would decay most swiftly—the stomach, intestines, liver, and lungs. They had also realized that a body needed to be dried out, and they had found a way to do this by using a material called natron. Natron is a kind of salt that occurs naturally in Egypt. It is a mixture of sodium carbonate and sodium bicarbonate, often called washing soda and baking soda. The embalmers used natron to preserve bodies. They also used it to preserve the organs they removed, which were placed in stone jars for burial in the tomb.

A treated body was little more than a skeleton covered with leathery skin. Around 2400 B.C. embalmers began trying to make the body look more as it had in life. They molded a shell of linen and plaster over the body and painted it in lifelike colors. Later some embalmers used resin. They melted this sticky stuff, which came from cone-bearing trees of Lebanon, and poured it over the body to form a shell. As it happened, the resin sealed out bacteria and moisture and helped to preserve the body.

This was the start of mummy making in Egypt, and the ancient Egyptians went on making mummies for another 3,000 years. During this time the art of embalming had many ups and downs. It flourished in periods when Egypt was strong, united, and prosperous. It declined in periods of civil war, invasions, famines, and the breaking of trade links with Lebanon. During these times even royal bodies were poorly preserved. Mummy making finally came to an end in the fourth century A.D., by which time most of the people had adopted Christianity. In this faith the body did not have to be preserved to ensure eternal life. So the practice of making mummies ended. People were simply buried in the clothes they had worn in life.

The art of embalming reached its peak during a period known as the New Kingdom (1570–1070 B.C.) and in the years immediately following. Many beautifully preserved bodies have survived from this period. Yet it has taken modern scientists years to work out how the bodies were treated. The chief reason is that no Egyptian account of embalming has ever been found. There are accounts of burial rituals, which mention that embalming took 70 days. But there is no known step-by-step account. The only full accounts come from foreigners. One of the best was written by the Greek historian Herodotus, who visited Egypt in the fifth century B.C. It is interesting and helpful, but there is no way of telling whether it is wholly accurate.

To learn about mummy making in ancient Egypt, scientists have looked for evidence in many mummies. Using clues from these studies, several scientists set up experiments to see if they too could make mummies, using mice, rats, pigeons, and ducks. The experiments solved several problems.

One very important question had to do with how the bodies were dried out. Chemical tests showed the presence of natron. Herodotus also says that bodies were placed in natron. But what form was the natron in—was it dry or dissolved in water? Experiments showed that embalmers must have packed bodies in large amounts of dry natron; when dissolved in liquid, natron did not do the job. They also showed that 30 to 40 days is the time needed to dry

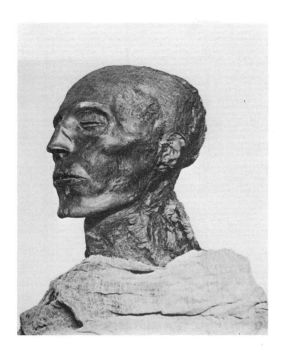

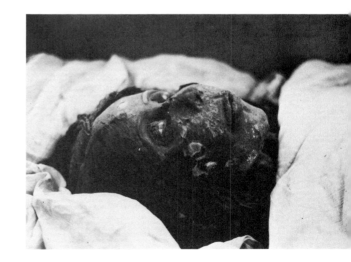

ABOVE LEFT: The mummy of Seti I is one of the most lifelike known.

ABOVE RIGHT: Countless horror movies have been inspired by the mummy of Rameses III.

RIGHT: The mummy of Queen Nodjme illustrates some of the changes that took place in mummy making during the New Kingdom and the period immediately following. The embalmers braided her hair, gave her artificial eyes, and padded out her cheeks and limbs.

[31]

out a body, no matter what its size.

Herodotus, however, says that bodies were placed in natron for 70 days. It is possible that he was wrong. It is equally possible that this was true in the fifth century B.C., a time when embalming was in decline and the most important thing was the outward appearance of the body. Embalmers may have cut corners by using the same natron more than once. If so, drying a body would have taken more time.

Today it seems clear that there were several basic steps in the mummy making of ancient Egypt. Embalmers removed inner organs and preserved them. They washed the inside of the body with palm wine, which, as it happened, killed bacteria. They dried the body by packing it in dry natron for 40 days. Then they anointed it with oils, covered it with resin, and wrapped it in strips of linen cloth. Together with religious ceremonies, the whole process took 70 days.

By the time of the New Kingdom, embalmers were also removing the brain, usually through the nose with a hooked metal rod. Improvements were made in the appearance of bodies by padding them with resin-soaked rolls of bandages and linen pads. By 1200 B.C. another change took place. The embalmed internal organs were no longer buried in stone jars but were stuffed back into the body.

During the periods when it flourished in ancient Egypt, embalming was both an art and a science. The skill with which embalmers worked can be seen in mummies that have lasted thousands of years and now give scientists a window on life in ancient Egypt.

By the first and second centuries A.D., during the period of Roman rule, less attention was paid to preserving the body and more to outward appearances. Portraits painted on wooden panels took the place of plaster masks. These portraits are of a teenaged boy and of a young woman who is dressed in the Roman style.

The ancient Egyptians mummified animals
as well as human beings. Some were pets,
mummified because they were dearly loved
or to keep their owners company in the afterlife. Some were mummified for religious
reasons. The Egyptians worshipped many
gods and believed that certain animals
represented the gods in earthly forms.
Apparently, certain individual animals
were viewed as sacred; these were treated
royally and given royal funerals after
mummification. Other animal mummies
seem to have been offerings to the gods.
The cat-goddess Bastet had a huge and
devoted following. Pilgrims bought mummified cats to offer to the goddess at her
shrines. Large cemeteries filled with cat
mummies have been found near these
shrines. This wrapped mummy is unusual
because it was carefully made, but an x-ray
showed there was nothing inside—perhaps
this was an inexpensive offering, or perhaps
someone was cheated.

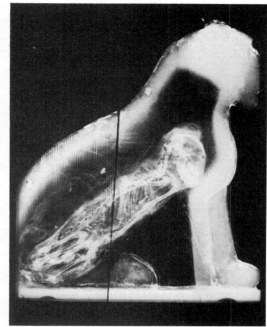

The coffin mirrors the shape of a cat, but the
x-ray picture shows that the animal inside
is only a kitten.

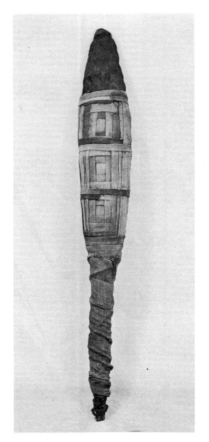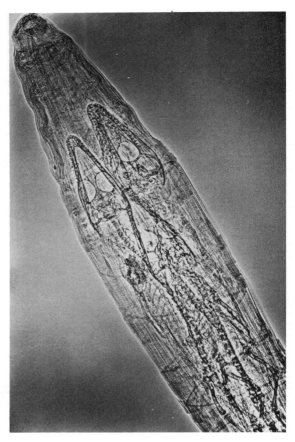

Crocodiles were also considered sacred. Herodotus wrote of a labyrinth where crocodiles with bejeweled feet were fed cakes and honeyed drinks in honor of the god Sobek. Some temples had pools of sacred crocodiles. When these crocodiles died, they were mummified. Here, what looks like the mummy of a big crocodile turned out in the x-ray to be three small ones.

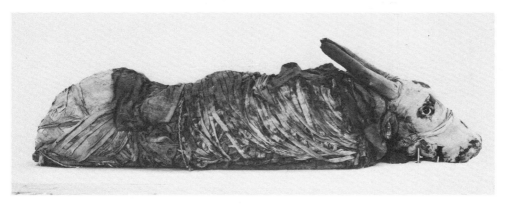

The most sacred animal was the Apis bull, believed to be the earthly form of the god who created all other gods. This Apis bull lived in luxury in a temple and was brought out, adorned in gold, for special festivals. In death, the bull was mummified and given a royal funeral. Then another Apis bull was chosen with exactly the same coloring and markings.

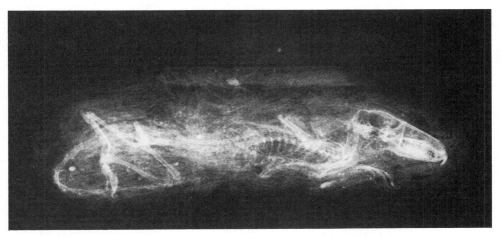

This strange-looking object was shown by x-rays to be a mummified gerbil with its own sack of food for the afterlife. It is not clear whether the gerbil had been a pet or whether it was a religious offering.

Makare, a high priestess, died when she was fairly young, either during childbirth or shortly thereafter. It was long thought that the child, a girl, also died and was buried with her mother. Now x-rays have shown that the small mummy in the tomb is not a child at all but a female baboon. Scholars do not know what became of the child or how to explain the baboon.

 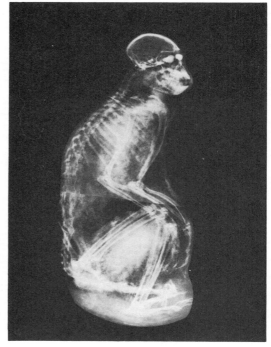

4. Seeing the Unseen

A single mummy can tell a lot about the life, health, and death of one person. The many, many mummies of ancient Egypt can tell about whole classes of people. What diseases did the Egyptians suffer from? How did diet affect their health? How long did they live? The answers to those and many other questions are in the mummies.

Getting at the answers was a problem for many years. One way to study mummies is to unwrap them and do an autopsy, but this destroys the mummies. Many mummies are too precious to destroy. Another way is to x-ray them. In the past this meant moving the mummies to hospitals or other places where the x-ray machines were. Many mummies were so fragile that moving them might have damaged them. Finally the development of a portable x-ray machine solved the problem. Now the machine can be taken to the mummies.

The x-ray pictures provide views of mummies never unwrapped—of pharaohs, queens, nobles, priests. The shape of the face appears, as do magic charms of gold and semiprecious stones within the wrappings. The pictures show that some mummies have been wrongly identified, that they cannot be the person they were thought to be. They have helped to clarify family relationships. They have produced some

Because the pharaohs of the New Kingdom were different physical types, x-rays offer one of the few means of identifying family relationships. These head x-rays of Amenhotep II and his son Thutmosis IV show a close similarity in the jaws and the shapes of the skulls. These and other photographs in this book were taken by Dr. James E. Harris of the University of Michigan's School of Dentistry, who led a number of expeditions to Egypt to photograph and x-ray the royal mummies.

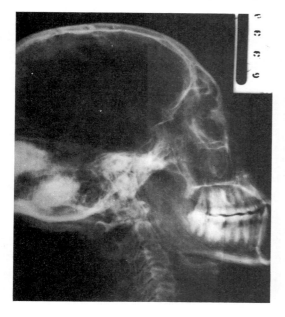 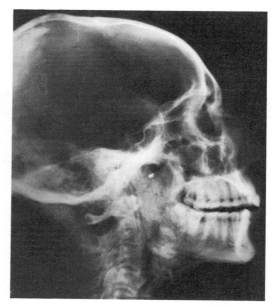

surprises and puzzles. Most of all, they have yielded important information about health in ancient Egypt. In the bones medical scientists can read age at death, signs of disease, fractures that healed.

X-rays show that the Egyptians suffered from many diseases known in the modern world—tuberculosis, polio, ar-

Who is he? One of the best preserved royal mummies was thought to be that of Thutmosis I. According to history, he led Egypt back to glory during the ten years of his reign and died in 1512 B.C. at the age of 50. However, the long bones of the legs, as shown in x-rays, appear to be those of someone younger than eighteen. Is history wrong—was Thutmosis I really a child-king? Or did he perhaps suffer a disease that kept his bones from maturing naturally? Or is the mummy that of someone else? So far, no one can say.

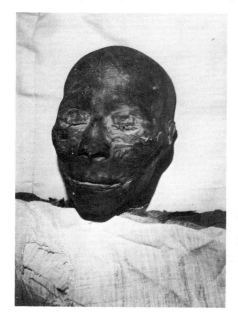

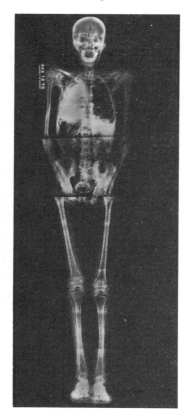

[41]

thritis, gallstones, hardening of the arteries. They also show that the most serious health problems arose from the environment, from the Nile and the desert.

The Nile was the lifeblood of Egypt. Its yearly floods dropped soil that enriched the river valley. Its waters, drawn off in canals, irrigated fields and pastures. From the fields came barley and wheat, fruits, vegetables, herbs. The cattle grazing the pastures supplied milk and eventually became meat on the tables of the rich. There were wild fowl to trap in the marshes of the Nile and fish from the river itself. The many tomb paintings of banquets and lists of grave foods make clear that the Egyptians enjoyed food and drink and that they ate well.

But the life-giving river was also a source of disease. It was a source of waterborne parasites—small animals that invade another creature, using its body as a place to live and feed but doing nothing that benefits the host. Most of the parasites that infected the ancient Egyptians were worms with complicated life cycles. But in general they spent part of their lives in human hosts and part in fresh water—canals,

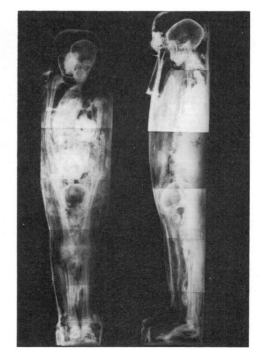

The Mummy with Two Skulls

At the time of her death, Lady Tashat was married and was also one of the few educated women of her day. That much could be learned from the writing on her coffin. In 1975 the Minneapolis Institute of Arts decided to x-ray the mummy, and a strange story began to unfold. Lady Tashat had been about fifteen when she died—the ends of the long bones of her legs had not closed, as they would have if she had been older. For unknown reasons, her body was twisted and had a number of broken bones. To the great surprise of the investigators, there appeared to be a second skull, which had been placed between the mummy's legs. Their best guess was that the embalmer had made a mistake.

There the matter rested until recently, when the mummy was examined again, this time with a CAT scanner. A CAT scanner passes an x-ray beam through a body from many different angles; a computer then translates the information into images on a video screen. The results are far more detailed and precise than those in a regular x-ray picture. The CAT scan deepened the mystery of Lady Tashat.

She had had an infection in her knee and hip at the time she died, but this would not have killed her. In addition to broken bones, the mummy had slashes across the soles of the feet. Yet even these injuries should not have caused her death—and may have occurred after death. At present no one can say how she died.

The second skull appeared to be that of a grown man. It had been carefully embalmed and wrapped, and appears to have been placed with Lady Tashat's body on purpose. The back of the skull had been beaten in, although it was not clear whether this had happened before or after death. The second skull remains a puzzle. Extra bones have been found with other mummies, but they usually turn out to be chicken bones—apparently the remains of the embalmer's lunch.

wet fields, marshes. Some kinds invaded their hosts through the skin, some were swallowed in drinking water. All caused misery, such as sores, rashes, and a growing weakness over a number of years. The remains of parasites and their eggs appear in x-rays of many mummies. They were a major reason why the life span of the average Egyptian was 35 to 40 years.

At the edge of the Nile Valley was the desert. Its dust storms filled the air with tiny particles of sand. The sand scarred the lungs of the Egyptians, and its effect on their teeth was equally serious.

The chief dental problem among the ancient Egyptians was extreme wear. It showed in the teeth of skeletons and mummies that medical scientists had examined earlier. Now

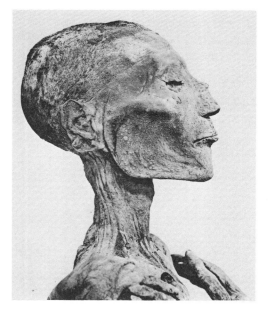

Studying the small blister-like marks on his face, scientists decided that Rameses V had had smallpox and may have died of it.

This wooden model of a granary found in a tomb shows workers filling sacks with grain to be emptied into storage bins. Because it almost never rains in Upper Egypt, the granary had no roof—and that was one route by which sand got into the grain.

the x-rays of pharaohs, priests, and nobles showed that their teeth too had rapidly worn down. The only possible explanation was sand. Somehow sand from the desert must have got into the food. As the Egyptians chewed, particles of sand ground down their teeth.

How that much sand got into their food was something of a puzzle until 1971. In that year the Manchester Museum in England was having an Egyptian exhibition. Among the displays were a large number of pieces of ancient Egyptian bread. X-rays showed that each piece contained vast quantities of mineral fragments. Some of the minerals were kinds that came from the soil in which the grain had grown. Some came from the kind of stones used to grind the grain. But most of the fragments were the pure quartz of desert sand. Dust storms must have added sand to grain when it was being harvested, winnowed, and stored. The sand went into bread along with the flour. Because the Egyptians ate large amounts of bread, they also chewed large amounts of sand.

Sometimes sand may have been added on purpose. A scientist at the Manchester Museum tried making flour with ancient Egyptian grinding stones. After 15 minutes of work, the grain was still whole. But when he did what other ancient peoples are reported to have done and added sand to the grain, he was quickly able to make fine flour.

Sand in their daily bread caused serious tooth problems for peasants and pharaohs alike. It wore down the hard parts of their teeth, the outside enamel and the underlying dentine. In some people new dentine formed. In most, teeth wore down faster than new dentine could form. Then the inside of the tooth was exposed. This is the pulp chamber, which houses the nerves and blood supply for the tooth. Without dentine as a barrier, disease-causing bacteria could invade the tooth's root canals. Painful infections followed and sometimes led to death.

Both the Nile and the desert were sources of health problems, as x-ray pictures make clear. The same pictures have revealed much else about life and health in ancient Egypt.

The servants in this wooden model are making bread: grinding grain, shaping dough, and readying a loaf for baking. The grinding added tiny fragments of stone to the flour. Sand may have been added to help the grinding process.

Even so, there are many details that x-rays do not show, and that is why scientists welcome the chance to do an autopsy, to make an in-depth study of a mummy. One of the most interesting autopsies was performed by a team of scientists at the Manchester Museum in 1975 on a mummy known as No. 1770.

The work begins. Members of the Manchester
University team, led by Dr. Rosalie David,
start the unwrapping of mummy No. 1770.

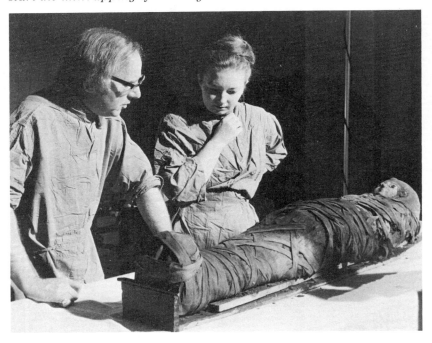

5. Mummy No. 1770

Museums have a limited number of mummies. Every time one is unwrapped, the number grows smaller, and so autopsies are not often performed. But sometimes a museum has a mummy that is not important to its collection. This is a mummy it does not want to display and a mummy about which almost nothing is known. As it happened, the Manchester Museum had just such a mummy. Its wrappings were in poor condition and no one knew what period it dated from, where it was found, or who the dead person was. The mummy was known only by its museum number, 1770. This was the mummy the museum made available to a team of scientists who wanted to use modern techniques to study the wrappings and body in detail.

It was also a mummy with a mystery. X-rays taken years earlier had shown the mummy was that of a young person.

The lower parts of the legs were missing, and close to the leg bones was a rounded object. The x-rays did not reveal what it was, but its shape suggested a baby's head. Was this the mummy of a mother and child? Had the mother died shortly after giving birth? Was she perhaps an unwed mother who had been punished with a violent death? Those were questions the scientists wondered about as they began their work.

After new x-rays were taken, the unwrapping began. Insect remains found in the bandages were carefully removed for later study. As pieces of cloth were lifted away, the lower part of the mask came into view. Beneath it were the bare bones of the neck and skull. These were in small pieces, but even so, once the pieces had been cleaned it was possible to see that the left side of the nose had been damaged by the iron hook the embalmers had used to remove the brain. The team was surprised to see red and blue paint on the skull bones. How and why had the bones been exposed?

Gently removing more cloth, the scientists found the mummy's arms were crossed on the chest and the hands had gold fingertip covers. The inner organs had been removed and the space filled with bandages and mud. The organs themselves were missing.

A small, hard object that had appeared in the x-rays proved to be a Guinea worm, a parasite that is taken in with drinking water. Within a human host, the young forms of Guinea worm develop into adults. The adults mate, and the male dies. The female, which may grow three feet long, wanders through the tissues under the skin. She generally comes to

X-ray pictures of 1770's legs showed a mysterious mass, which the team thought might be a baby.

The mummy had a painted face mask and, under the wrappings, a chest mask.

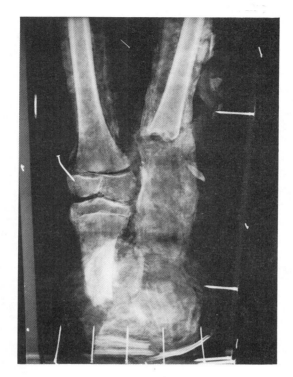

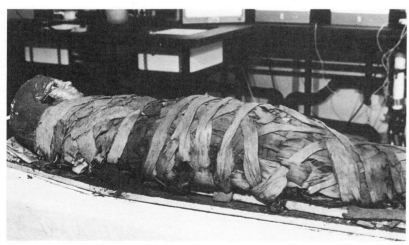

rest in the legs or feet of the host. There blisters form. They burst on contact with fresh water. The female's eggs are released into the water, and the life cycle starts again. If invaded by bacteria, the blisters may form dangerous sores.

When the Manchester team unwrapped the legs of mummy 1770, they found, as the x-rays had shown, that both legs had been amputated, the left below the knee and the right above the knee. The mummy's right leg had been lengthened with a piece of wood to make it the same length as the left. The wood had been splinted to the leg bone. This meant there could not have been much, if any, flesh on the bone when the splinting was done. The feet were artificial and had gold toenail covers. The right foot was made of reeds and mud, with the ends of the reeds serving as toes. The left foot was simply a mass of reeds and mud.

By now the scientists could see that there was not even a trace of a baby. The rounded shape that had shown in the x-rays was actually a pair of beautiful slippers that had been placed on the soles of the feet.

In one way mummy 1770 was disappointing—it was very poorly preserved. No one could even be certain of its sex, although members of the team came to feel that the young person had been a girl and spoke of the mummy as female. Very little skin, muscle, or soft tissue were left, and the bones of the skull and lower trunk were broken. The scientists could not tell when the fractures had occurred. In a living person, tissue called callus forms at the place where a bone is broken. It holds the bone together until the fracture

*The "baby"
turned out to be
decorated sandals
placed over
false feet.*

heals. Callus in a recently dead person shows that the fracture occurred during life. But callus thick enough to last thousands of years would take several weeks to form. So if there is no callus in a mummy—and there was none in 1770— there was no way to tell whether the fracture occurred after death or shortly before. The scientists suspected, however, that the bones were broken after death. The damaged mask and the lack of jewelry and charms spoke of tomb robbers and rough handling.

In other ways, mummy 1770 was both interesting and puzzling. The evidence indicated that the body had been in a state of considerable decay when the embalmers worked on it. The wooden leg was attached to bone. All the internal organs were missing and so was the left kneecap, which suggested that the ligaments holding it in place had rotted away. The red and blue paint on the skull bones was a sign that the hair and scalp had been missing.

Why had the body decayed? Why were the legs amputated? The scientific team could think of various explanations.

One had to do with the Guinea worm. Perhaps infections had cut off the flow of blood to the legs and feet. In an effort to save the girl's life, doctors had amputated her legs, but the patient died. But if that was the case, why hadn't she been promptly embalmed?

Or perhaps the legs had been cut off in an accident, such as the collapse of a building. If the girl had been buried in rubble and not found for some time, that might explain the decay.

Or suppose the girl had drowned in the Nile, where decay would set in quickly. The body might have been attacked by a hippopotamus. Although hippos are plant eaters, they are likely to attack floating objects that appear threatening. One bite from a hippo could easily cut off a pair of legs.

A crocodile was another possibility, because it would certainly attack a floating body. The problem with this idea was that crocodiles do not usually bite through bones. They are much more likely to grasp an arm or a leg in their huge jaws and shake it until it tears loose. On the other hand, a crocodile attack might explain why the embalmers went to so much trouble over a body that was hauled out of the Nile—why they made a face and chest mask, lengthened a leg, made artificial feet, applied gold covers to the fingers and toes. The ancient Egyptians, believing that crocodiles were earthly forms of gods, considered anyone who became food for them to be sacred.

As things turned out, there was another explanation for the state of the body and it took everyone by surprise. When the carbon-14 dating was completed, it showed that the mummy was far older than its wrappings. The wrappings dated to a time when the Romans ruled Egypt, around A.D. 260. The mummy's bones dated to around 1000 B.C. This meant that 1770 was a mummy that had been wrapped twice. It had been preserved and wrapped after the girl died, then rewrapped more than a thousand years later. Now some pieces of the puzzle began to fall into place.

There was no need to explain why the corpse had decayed, because it hadn't. Rather, it was the mummy that had been damaged by water and then had decayed. The soft tissues of the body were probably missing because they had stuck to the original wrappings.

The way the second embalmers had prepared the body made clear that they did not know whether they were dealing with a male or a female. This meant they did not know the mummy's identity. But the trouble they took shows that they thought they were dealing with someone of importance. The tomb from which the mummy came must have led them to that conclusion. At times in ancient Egypt royal mummies were moved to new tombs. If they had been damaged, they were repaired at the time of the move. Quite possibly 1770 was a person of royal or noble birth whose mummy was damaged when a tomb was flooded.

The Manchester team carried out many other investigations of 1770. They studied the mummy's wrappings to find out what they were made of, how they had been woven, what sort of gum had been used as an adhesive. More x-rays were taken. And the many insect remains were studied. They showed, among other things, that flies had had a chance to feed on the mummy and to breed. This finding was further evidence that the mummy had been wet before it was repaired and rewrapped.

Flies lay eggs, which hatch out into wormlike creatures called larvae. In time a kind of case forms around each larva. Inside, the soft matter of the larva breaks down and turns into an adult fly. If larva cases are found in mummies or their wrappings, it is a sign that flies have bred there. It is also a sign that the mummies and wrappings have been wet, because the larvae cannot eat dry food. Flies lay their eggs only on moist food sources.

While some members of the team were working with insect remains, x-rays, and wrappings, others were studying 1770's skull and teeth.

X-rays had shown that the mummy's wisdom teeth had not yet grown in, and so the girl must have been less than 20 years old. The dentist on the team now examined the roots of the second molars. Their stage of development told him that 1770 had been 13 to 14 years old. He was surprised to see that the teeth showed no sign of being worn down by sand. He also found that two teeth in the upper jaw were oddly placed. A space between them near the gum formed a trap for food particles. Usually such a trap leads to infection, which damages the bone of the jaw. But this had not happened to 1770. The lack of wear and damage suggested that her diet was soft, perhaps mostly liquid. Or she may have swallowed food without trying to chew it much. Most likely she had not been very healthy.

She must also have breathed mainly through her mouth. The badly formed bones in the inner part of her nose would have made it almost impossible to breathe any other way. If a person always breathes through the mouth, the gums around the upper front teeth become irritated and the bone behind them pitted. Pits in the bones of 1770's mouth showed that she had indeed breathed through her mouth.

By this time the Manchester team had learned a great deal about 1770. She was a young person who had lived a short life with considerable suffering. She had had to breathe through her mouth, had sore gums, ate only liquid or soft food, and had been infected by Guinea worms, which cause fever and an itching rash as well as blisters. Finally, by means still not clear, she had lost her legs around the time she died.

One final step remained to be taken—to find out what 1770 had looked like. The skull had broken into about 30 pieces, some of them very small and fragile. The pieces lay in a

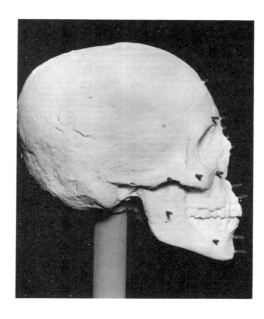

The pegs indicate the probable thickness of soft tissues of the face.

jumbled heap and were mixed with mud and bandages. Once the pieces of bone had been cleaned, one member of the team made casts of them in plastic. When the plastic pieces were fitted together, much of the left side of the skull was still missing. A plaster cast was made to fill out the basic shape of the head. Now small pegs were placed in the plastic skull and cut to precise lengths. Each showed how thick the soft tissues of the face would be on a 13-year-old person. The face was then built up with modeling clay. First it took on a general human appearance. Then it took on an appearance of its own, shaped by the underlying bones. This model was used to cast the head in wax, so that changes could be made if more was learned about 1770. The wax head was painted, given glass eyes, a wig, and eyelashes. And there at last was

The finished head showed an attractive young girl.

1770—an attractive teenager, perhaps of royal or noble birth, who had laughed, cried, and lived 3,000 years ago.

With 1770 and other mummies, modern scientists have learned a great deal about life and death in ancient Egypt. But the studies have been mostly of royalty, nobles, priests, and the wealthy. In the time of the Old Kingdom only royalty and the highest nobles were mummified. Later the wealthy were also mummified. Not until late in the history of ancient Egypt were ordinary people allowed to have their dead preserved, if they could afford it. As a result, most mummies come from the upper classes. And that is one reason why various scientists are interested in studying the ancient civilizations of Peru. In those, almost everyone became a mummy.

[61]

An adult male mummy of Peru, from sometime in the 500-year period before the Spanish conquest. Notice the tattooing on the right wrist and the cords that were used to hold the body with its knees bent up.

6. The Telltale Mummies of Peru

At the time of the Spanish conquest, in the 1530s, the Inca Empire stretched 3,000 miles along the western coast of South America, taking in parts of what are now Ecuador, Peru, Bolivia, and Chile. The empire itself was young, but it united many ancient city-states and linked them with roads. Although the people could not read or write, they had built cities of stone, palaces, temples. Farmers worked terraced lands in the mountains, irrigated lands along the coast. Miners dug out ore bearing gold, silver, copper, and tin. Craftsmen turned metals into fine ornaments and jewelry. They made beautiful pottery and wove some of the loveliest cloth ever seen.

There was much to wonder at—and plunder—in the Inca Empire, but the conquerors were most astonished by the mummies. In this empire all classes of people were mummified after death. A common Indian was then buried in a simple grave with his few possessions. A local nobleman was usually placed in a tomb with several chambers. With him were the bodies of some of his wives, servants, and followers, who had been chosen to serve him after death. They had been killed and mummified.

The treatment of the Inca rulers was the most astounding of all. After being mummified, a body was placed in the royal funeral tomb, along with quantities of fine cloth woven for the ceremony in all four quarters of the empire. Food and drink were also placed in the tomb, as were the ruler's weapons, his symbols of office, and all his used clothing. Llamas were sacrificed, and so were some of the ruler's wives and followers. When ceremonies ended in the Inca capital of Cuzco, the mummies were taken over by the dead ruler's family and cared for by special attendants. They knew when to offer the mummy food and drink. They whisked away flies, changed and washed the mummy's clothing, and sent for visitors to whom the mummy wished to speak. For at least a year, the royal mummy was treated as if it were alive. After that it was placed in a great hall where the other royal mummies were kept, each seated on his throne.

Several times a year the royal mummies were brought out and carried through the streets to mark special events and festivals. One Spanish account says: "The bodies were intact:

Drawing in a Spanish source of around 1613 portrays the bodies of an Inca king, his queen, and a servant being carried on a litter to Cuzco for burial.

not even hair, eyelashes, or eyebrows were missing. They were dressed as during life, the royal fringe on their heads, and were seated as in the Indian custom with their hands crossed over their chests, the right over the left, eyes down, as if looking at the ground. . . . The bodies weighed so little that any Indian could carry them from house to house in his arms or on his shoulders. . . ."

The mummies of the Inca rulers served an important purpose in the empire. They were proof that earlier rulers had really existed and that the family owning them was of direct descent. They strengthened the claim of a ruler to his throne. Like all the other mummies, they were also part of religious beliefs. The grave goods buried with mummies make clear that people believed in a life after death. The mummies seem to have served as a link between the living and the dead.

Some of the royal mummies were burned by the Spanish conquerors. Others were still being exhibited in Lima 50 years after the conquest, but no one knows what became of them. Nor does anyone know how the royal bodies were preserved.

One Spanish account of the conquest says that mummies were made simply by drying bodies in the open air. Many mummies probably were, since for hundreds of years the Indians had been preserving meat this way. It is possible too that mummies were made by different methods in different parts of Peru. In the desert that runs along the coast, mummies may have been made by burying bodies in the hot, dry sands. Some tribes learned to make mummies another way—

Pottery figures from the north Peruvian coast are carrying a coffin and mummy in a funeral procession.

Some 5,000 years ago, fishing tribes on the coast of northern Chile practiced artificial mummification, especially with the bodies of infants and children. They removed the brain and internal organs and stiffened the trunk, arms, and legs with sticks. The body of this child was then coated with a thin layer of clay and some paint, wrapped in a cloak of bird skins, and given a wig of human hair.

to remove the soft parts of a body and then dry it with heat or fire and cure it with smoke. Archeologists need to study and date many more mummies before they can learn the whole story of mummy making in Peru.

They know, however, that mummy making in Peru and northern Chile goes back at least 5,000 years. And they think that the idea of making mummies probably arose from the discovery that bodies put in certain places were preserved. This must have happened in the cool, dry caves of the highlands. It must also have happened in the desert that runs along the coast of Peru and northern Chile. The region is probably the driest place in the world, but here and there it is slashed by small rivers that flow down the Andes Mountains toward the sea. The rivers create oases. The earliest settlers of the river valleys may well have saved the good land for farming and buried their dead in the desert sands.

In time cities and civilizations developed around some of these river valleys. The cities are long abandoned, but the dry climate has preserved their ruins. It has preserved embroidered cloth, pottery, metal ornaments, and even pots of beans, corn, and other crops that are thousands of years old.

With the growth of cities came changes in burial customs. By 400 B.C. a big change had taken place in southern Peru. Where cities were growing, large burial grounds were also taking shape. These were underground cities of the dead. Each grave had an opening, or shaft, that reached 18 or 20 feet into the ground. At the bottom was a chamber in which groups of the dead were seated. Each body rested in a coiled basket or in a gourd, with its knees drawn up. It was covered with layers of cloth, forming a mummy bundle about five feet high.

The making of mummy bundles went on for some 2,000 years, as did simpler burials. These mummies are important to scientists because they cover a long span of time. They offer a chance to study life and health both before and after the Spanish conquest.

For several thousand years one group of people—the Indians—lived in the coastal and highland valleys. In the 1530s another racial group—the Spaniards—arrived and conquered them. What diseases did the Indians have before the arrival of the Spaniards? What diseases did they acquire from their conquerors? What was the state of their health before and after the conquest? Did they eat as well after the conquest? Did they live as long? Did their causes of death change? The mummies hold the answers.

Most of the studies so far have been made by one group of American and Peruvian scientists. Since 1970 they have been working in the Peruvian state named Ica, about 180 miles south of Lima. Here the river valleys, which are about 25 miles long and a few miles wide, were centers of civilization long before the Spaniards arrived. Here warrior-farmers raised corn, potatoes, fruits, beans, manioc, and grain in irrigated fields. Here cities developed in the desert, as did underground cities of the dead. In these cemeteries the scientists dig for mummies. Each year they have found and examined 50 to 75.

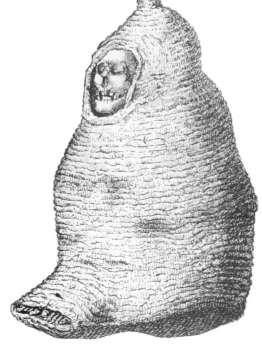

The passing of time brought changes in the ways bundles were prepared. For one thing, they were given false heads made of fibers and cloth and often painted red. Shells or pieces of metal served as eyes. A nose might be made of wood and sewn on to the head, which was topped with a wig made of human hair or plant fibers. A false head might wear a woven cap or a brightly colored headband.

Mummies of adults were seated on a coiled cotton disk, knees drawn tight against the chest, hands opened flat over the face. They were covered with layers of cotton and cloth, then bound with wrapping cords. Often the cords covered the whole body, leaving openings only for the face and the toes. At the end a kind of dress or tunic was placed on the bundle. The final mummy bundle often weighed 200 to 300 pounds.

One of the first things they noticed was that over the last 5,000 years the people of Ica have not changed much in height. Today's people are of mixed blood—Indian, Spanish, and African—but they are still about the same size as their Indian ancestors. In Europe and North America people are much bigger than their ancestors—suits of armor look to us as if they had been made for boys instead of men. The difference is probably in diet: We eat better than our ancestors did. The Ica do not.

The scientists were curious about how long people had lived. Today in countries where people eat well and have good medical care, the average life span is more than 70 years. In the rest of the world it is less than 40 years. To learn about the ancient people of Ica, medical scientists studied x-rays of their teeth and bones. They found that before the beginning of Spanish rule, 27 percent of the people lived to be more than 40. In colonial times only 12 percent did. Both before and during colonial rule only 50 percent of all children lived to be ten or more.

How healthy had the adults been as children? To find out, the team of scientists again turned to x-rays. They were looking for certain kinds of scars, called Harris lines, in the long bones of adult mummies. These scars form when a child lacks food or is sick in bed for a short time. Bone growth stops but the end of a bone goes on laying down calcium. When the child recovers or the food shortage ends, bone growth begins again. But the line formed by the calcium may remain. Its distance from the end of the bone can be used to estimate the person's age when bone growth stopped.

These studies showed that 5,000 years ago the healthiest children lived on the coast. Their diet of seafood was high in protein. The children in mountain villages ate less protein and lived in more crowded conditions, where diseases may have spread more readily. By the time of the Spanish conquest, however, the children in mountain villages were healthier than the coastal children, and no one knows why. Perhaps there was a change in diet, perhaps in disease.

Long before colonial rule there were at least two forms of tuberculosis in Peru. A number of mummies show signs of a kind that affects bone and of a kind that is carried by the blood to many parts of the body. Both are caused by bacteria that can come from people, mammals, birds, fish, and snakes.

Tuberculosis of the lungs seems to have been brought to the New World by Europeans, and it killed huge numbers of Indians in both North and South America.

The team of scientists was also looking for parasites in mummies. Their work settled an old argument about hookworm: Was it brought to the Americas with African slaves or was it present earlier? The team found hookworm in a mummy buried sometime between A.D. 890 and 950. Although more hookworm came with the slaves, the first proba-

An eight-year-old boy was among the mummies of Ica studied by the team of American and Peruvian scientists, led by Dr. Marvin J. Allison of the Medical College of Virginia. Tuberculosis had affected the boy's spine, and for some time before his death he had not been able to walk. Someone had made him a special seat of sun-dried clay and straw, shaped it to fit his body, and lined it with a thick cloth cushion to make him comfortable.

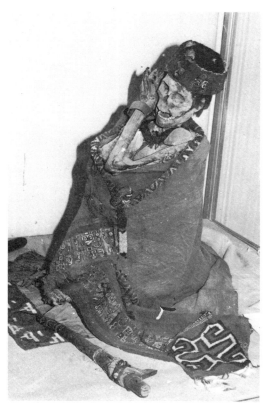

This is the mummy that settled the question about hookworm.

bly arrived with the ancestors of the Indians, who came from Asia at at a time when a land bridge linked it with North America.

Another interesting discovery was that a number of mummies showed signs of skull surgery—a piece of the bony skull had been scraped away or cut out. Healed openings showed that many patients had survived the operation, and some had been operated on more than once.

There was no sign, though, that anything had been done

*Adult male mummy
has its knees drawn up,
hands open against the face.*

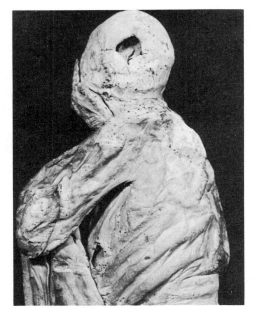

*The side view shows
clear signs of skull surgery.
The small black spots
are holes made by insects.*

about toothaches. Before the coastal people became farmers, they had few cavities or jaw infections. Their chief problem was that they wore down their teeth, by using them to open clams and oysters and by eating sandy food. Most people had worn their teeth down to the gums by the age of 25. Later, as farmers, they ate foods that were high in sugars and starches. Children had many cavities. Adults also had bone infections and lost many teeth. Toothaches must have been common and painful.

Modern methods make it possible to study the blood groups of mummies. Using markers found in blood cells, the scientists are starting to trace the movements of ancient tribes as they moved from one valley to another. Using blood groups and grave goods, they can identify relatives among the mummies in a cemetery. Blood groups also tell about the mixing of races after the arrival of the Spaniards.

That arrival caused drastic changes in the Indians' way of life. The only written accounts of what happened are Spanish. To find out how true these are, the team of scientists turned to mummies and the tales they have to tell. One year they excavated a colonial cemetery in the Pisco Valley.

They chose the valley because it had been a busy place in colonial times. Its road linked the coastal roads with mountain roads, and the mountain roads led to important mines. Mines were what most interested the Spaniards, once they had plundered the Inca Empire. The scientists reasoned that the Pisco Valley road must have been much traveled and that

Indians and Spaniards must have been in close contact in the valley.

The team opened 72 tombs, dating from 1580 to 1630 and later. In every one they found only the old Indian ways of burial. They were surprised, because Spanish accounts of the conquest tell of great efforts to convert the Indians to Christianity. Yet there was no evidence of this among the tombs and mummies. The scientists decided that the Spaniards had been most interested in the Indians as a source of cheap labor.

The mummies support that idea. They also support the accounts Spanish priests wrote telling of the terrible cruelty with which the Indians were treated.

The Spaniards wanted silver, and they needed men to mine it. They taxed each village or region and collected the tax in the form of labor. At first they required all able-bodied men to work in the mines for three months of the year. Conditions were so bad that many miners died. The Spanish rulers then increased the length of time the men had to work in the mines. With the men away, village farming was neglected, and many Indians lacked food.

The mummies of the Pisco Valley cemetery reflected this. It was clear that the people had been poor and short of food. There were few grave goods and little food in the tombs. Also, the clothes of the Indians had been patched, then patched again. Most of the mummies were females. They outnumbered the males by 15 to 1. The few male mummies usually showed handicaps that had made them unfit for hard labor. Most of the village men had been sent away and had never returned. Apparently they had been sent to the mines. Small lumps of molten silver found in the tombs point to a connection with the silver mines and the places where silver ore was refined.

The mummies in this same cemetery had many broken bones. The scientists found nearly 500 times as many fractures as they had among mummies of earlier periods. Nearly every mummy had several fractures in different stages of healing, most often broken ribs and collarbones. One woman alone had 13 broken ribs. Illustrations in one Spanish account show kneeling Indian servants being kicked by Spanish masters. Such treatment may explain the many broken bones.

Spanish records draw a grim picture of the mines. These began at the surface and followed veins of silver into the ground, often for hundreds of feet. There the tunnels were roughly shored up, but cave-ins happened almost daily. Because there were no air shafts, the air was thick with dust and gases. Ore was carried out of the mines in 50-pound sacks on the backs of miners, who often had to climb 500 to 1,000 feet on woven ladders.

Mummies again support the Spanish accounts. Examining 12 mummies of miners, the scientists found the lungs contained silver, copper, iron, and other minerals. With their lungs weakened, 3 had caught tuberculosis and 10 had caught pneumonia and died of it. The stress placed on their bodies also showed in their joints and hearts.

Mining in colonial times killed more Indians than all disease epidemics together. In 1629 the Spaniards sent 80,000 Indians to the mines. Forty-five years later they could find only 1,674 able-bodied men for the mines.

The mummies bear silent witness to what happened. They are direct evidence of what Indian life was like under Spanish rule. The story they tell supports some written accounts and casts doubt on others.

Such direct evidence is important. It offers a way of measuring and testing the truth of what has been written. And that is one of the chief reasons why scientists half a world away have been studying a very different group of mummies, found in the peat bogs of Denmark.

The Tollund man's head was so well preserved that even his eyebrows and the stubble of his beard were intact. His pointed cap was made of eight pieces of sheepskin sewn together and fastened under the chin with a thong of hide tied in a bowknot.

7.   The Bog Bodies

In May 1950 two farmers were cutting peat for fuel near the village of Tollund in Denmark. They had dug down some eight or nine feet into the bog when they came upon the body of a man. His face was so fresh and lifelike that the farmers thought they had discovered a recent murder victim. They called the police in the nearby town of Silkeborg.

When they heard how and where the body had been found, the police suspected that this was not a recent death but a very old one. They were almost certain that the peat cutters had found another of the bog bodies. They called the Silkeborg Museum and invited staff members to go with them to the bog.

There they found the well-preserved body of a man who looked as if he were asleep. He was lying on his side, knees drawn up, eyes closed, a peaceful expression on his face. He wore a pointed cap made of pieces of sheepskin and a belt made of hide. Otherwise he was naked. The cause of death became clear when a lump of peat was removed from beside his head. Around his neck was a noose made of two leather thongs. The Tollund man had been hanged, then placed in a pit in the bog. Markings showed that the pit was an ancient peat cutting.

The pattern was familiar. This was another of the people who lived in what is now Denmark between 500 B.C. and A.D. 400, a time that is called the Iron Age in northern Europe. This was another Iron Age person who, for some reason, had been put to death and placed in a bog. As it happened, the bog preserved his body and turned it into a mummy.

A peat bog usually marks a place where a lake formed about 10,000 years ago, at the end of the last ice age, when giant glaciers melted and their water filled deep hollows. As time passed, plants began to grow out over the lake. The chief plants were mosses called sphagnum, or peat moss. As old mosses died, they sank to the bottom of the lake and new ones took their place. Gradually the lake began to fill in, first around the edges, then farther out. In this way, layers of dead plants were packed down into a mass that was spongy on top and solid below. This mass is peat. Peat builds up slowly, but over hundreds of years it can become many feet deep.

Sphagnum has leaflike parts that are constructed in a special way. Only a few of their cells hold the green matter called chlorophyll that enables plants to make food. The

The Tollund man lay in a sleeping position, wearing only his cap and a belt.

The noose had cut a furrow in his neck, making it clear that he had been hanged.

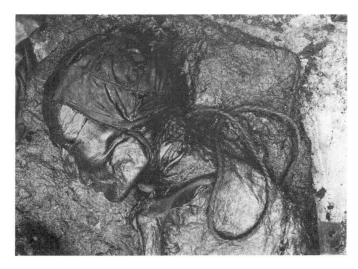

other cells are empty, and they have an extraordinary ability to take in and hold water. As a result, even if the whole lake has filled in, a peat bog is a very wet place.

Many people think that peat acts as a sponge and draws up groundwater, but this is not so. The deepest layers of peat are packed too tight for water to pass through. Only rainwater reaches the bog. The water in the bog contains minerals that were in the rainwater. And it contains acids that form naturally in a peat bog.

The tight packing means that there is little air—and little oxygen—in the bog. So there are not many oxygen-using bacteria. In addition, the acids greatly slow the action of bacteria in breaking down dead matter.

These facts explain why layers of peat can build up over hundreds of years. Unlike most dead plant matter, peat decays only a little.

The same facts explain why human bodies have been preserved in the peat bogs of northern Europe, from Ireland in the west to Russia in the east. Over the years some 2,000 bodies or parts of bodies have been found in these bogs, usually by peat cutters. A few were the bodies of people who had died fairly recently—airmen shot down during World War II, for example. Many were hundreds or thousands of years old and lay under many layers of peat, as the Tollund man did.

To preserve his body for study, the block of peat containing it was cut out of the bog, crated, and shipped to the National Museum in Copenhagen. There scientists examined it closely, x-rayed it, and did an autopsy.

Because bog acids have a tanning effect on skin, the Tollund man was dark brown. Museum scientists found that he had been 5 feet 3 inches tall and must have been at least 20 to 22 years old at the time of death, because his wisdom teeth had grown in. X-ray studies of the bones later showed that he had been 30 to 40 years old.

The autopsy showed that the Tollund man had eaten his last meal 12 to 24 hours before his death. It had been a thick soup made of grain and of weed seeds, ground in a hand mill and then boiled. The chief grains were two kinds of barley, and the soup also contained linseed oil. Water drunk with the meal must have come from the bog, because some sphagnum was also found in the stomach.

The soup was one clue to the time when the Tollund man lived. Linseed was not common in Denmark before 400 B.C. At that time the two kinds of barley—naked barley and covered barley—were also grown. But by A.D. 200 naked barley was no longer grown. Therefore the Tollund man must have eaten his last meal sometime between 400 B.C. and A.D. 200. Another clue was the place where he was found. His body had been in an Iron Age peat cutting, as scientists had seen at the time of its discovery. The kind of sphagnum under the body, they now found, was one that grew in the Iron Age. And a few days earlier an Iron Age wooden peat spade had been found nearby. Carbon-14 dating, which was done later, gave a death date of around 220 B.C.

The meal was also a clue to the time of year when the

Tollund man died. It must have been late winter or very early spring, a time when there were no fresh fruits, berries, herbs, or vegetables. The season helps to explain why the body was very well preserved. The best-preserved bodies happened to be placed in the bogs at a time when the temperature was close to freezing. The rapid chilling of a body slowed or stopped the action of the bacteria inside it, giving the acid water time to penetrate the body and preserve it. The best-preserved bodies also had no air—or oxygen—near them. That too was true of the Tollund man's. His body had been carefully placed in a pit, and a pit would be full of bog water.

In a way, the Tollund man added to the mysteries surrounding the bog bodies. Of those known to modern scientists, only his body was carefully placed in a sleeping position, eyes and mouth closed by someone. Only the Tollund man has a peaceful expression on his face. By contrast, three bodies from Borremose, to the north of Tollund, showed signs of violent handling.

The first Borremose body was found by peat cutters in 1946, about six feet down in the bog. It had been put in an Iron Age peat cutting in a sitting position. A birch branch had been placed above the body, probably to keep it from floating.

The peat bogs were lakes that filled in as dead plants—most of them peat moss—rained to the bottom. Today, peat cutting has ended in Denmark, and many of the bogs are being drained to make them fit for farming. There is little chance that more well-preserved bog bodies will be found there.

In 1938 the Elling woman was found about 300 feet from where the Tollund man was later found. Her hair was elaborately braided, and she was wearing a sheepskin cloak with the furred side in. A piece of oxhide, perhaps a cloak, was draped around her legs. Carbon-14 dating has shown that she was placed in the bog at about the same time as the Tollund man. Studies of x-rays and of her teeth show that she was about 30 years old and in good health, until she was hanged.

The Borremose man was hanged and placed in a peat bog around 840 B.C. The second Borremose body found has been dated to 475 B.C., the third to 770 B.C. The bog surrounds what was once a fortified Iron Age village. Quite possibly, all three persons lived in the village before being put to death.

The body was that of a man who was 5 feet 2 inches tall and clean-shaven. Both the hands and feet were well formed, and the hands did not look as if they had been used for hard labor. The Borremose man's last meal had been a thick soup of grains and seeds.

Scientists found that the back of the skull had been crushed sometime before the body was placed in the bog. The right thigh bone was broken, just above the knee, with part of the bone sticking out through the skin. This injury too had occurred before the bone was exposed to the acids in the bog water. The injuries may have played a part in the man's death, but they were probably not the cause of death. A hemp rope was pulled tight around his throat. Except for the rope, the Borremose man was naked, but two sheepskin capes were rolled up at his feet.

The following year another Borremose body was found, about half a mile from the first. The upper part of the body was naked, but the lower part was covered by a woolen blanket, a shawl, and a piece of cloth. The body was so badly decayed that no one could tell whether it was a man's or a woman's, but again the skull was crushed and the right leg bone broken, this time just below the knee. Around the neck was a leather thong with a yellow pearl and a bronze disk. Near the top of the body were some small bones belonging to a baby. Perhaps a mother and her infant were placed in the bog together.

In 1948 the remains of a plump woman lying on her stomach were found. Before being placed in the bog, her face had

The Grauballe man's body was carefully removed in a crated block of peat and taken to the museum.

been crushed and she had been scalped. The scalp, which had long hair, lay above the body in the bog. The body itself was lying on a woolen blanket and was naked.

The last well-preserved Danish bog body was found in 1952, by which time other fuels were replacing peat in farmhouses and peat cutting was coming to an end. This time peat cutters were working in a small bog near the village of Grauballe, when they uncovered a dark-skinned human head with short-cropped hair. The body was that of a man. He too was wholly naked.

Scientists who examined the body found that the Grauballe man's throat had been slit. He also had a broken shinbone

The Grauballe man, shown as he now appears, was the last of the bog bodies to be found in Denmark.

and a skull fracture caused by a blow from a blunt instrument. They could not tell whether he had been knocked unconscious before his throat was slit. The Grauballe man had been 5 feet 10 inches tall and in good health except for some arthritis in his spine.

The right hand and foot were so well preserved that their prints were still clear. The police studied them and discovered that the patterns were ones still found among the Danish people today. The condition of the hand showed that the Grauballe man had never done rough or heavy work.

He had a large mouth, but his teeth were small and heavily worn along the chewing edges, a sign that he was probably

The Grauballe man's right hand and foot were extremely well preserved. They make it clear that, whoever he was, he had never done rough or heavy work, such as farming or building.

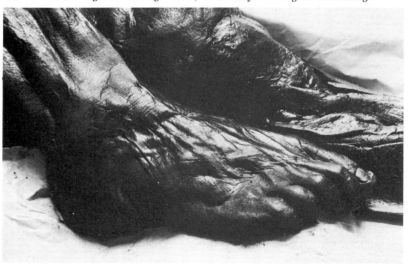

in his late 30s. One tooth had grown out of place and given him a bad bite. A number of missing teeth and cavities showed that he must have had some painful toothaches.

The Grauballe man had eaten his last meal just before he was killed. Like the Tollund man's, it had been a thick soup, but it contained more kinds of grains and seeds as well as some tiny pieces of bones, which may have come from the ribs of a small pig. It was also a much bigger meal than the Tollund man had eaten. Two kinds of seeds were from plants that grow only near the coast, which is some 30 miles from Grauballe. Perhaps he was killed near the coast, or perhaps there was trade in foodstuffs between the two regions. Possibly because of his bad bite, the Grauballe man did not chew his food very thoroughly. Two small stones and a piece of charcoal were also found in his stomach.

The ancient peat cutting in which the body was found showed that the Grauballe man had lived and died during the Iron Age. Carbon-14 dating places the time of his death around 55 B.C.

Studies of bog bodies show when and how these people were put to death, but they do not tell why. So far there is no clear-cut answer to that question. The Iron Age people had no written language, and so they left no records of their customs.

The only written accounts come from ancient Rome. Around the time of the birth of Christ, Roman armies tried, and failed, to conquer the Iron Age tribes of the north. Later a great deal of trade developed between the Romans and

Bog finds have made clear how the Iron Age women dressed. The clothing on the left consists of a checked skirt woven from wool, and a lambskin cape. The dress on the right is made from a single piece of tube-shaped cloth. The owner of the skirt had a horn comb in her pocket. The open-work cap came from the body of a young woman.

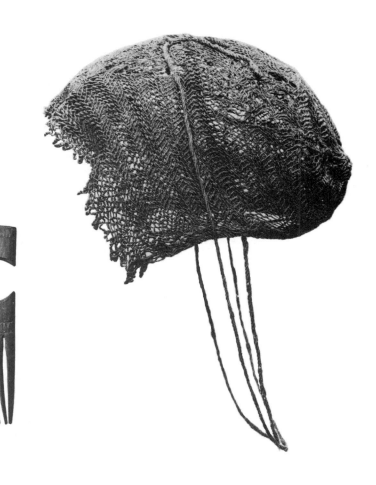

What the men wore is less clear. Roman accounts say they wore
only short sheepskin capes, like the ones found with the Borremose
man. This seems somewhat unlikely because the climate during the
Iron Age was cool and damp, and earlier men had been fully
dressed.

Northern men of the Iron Age wear capes, shirts, trousers, and tunics in this scene from the column of Marcus Aurelius in Rome, dating to about A.D. 193. It shows northern captives being forced to cut off one another's heads.

these people. Roman historians learned about the tribes from traders and soldiers and wrote about them. Their accounts, however, may not be wholly true. They were based on stories told by returning travelers, not on firsthand knowledge. Also, the Romans probably wished to present themselves in a favorable light as compared with the primitive people to the north. The Roman accounts are accepted only when backed up by archeological evidence.

The evidence shows that the Iron Age people of Denmark were peasants, who raised grains as well as cows, sheep, goats, pigs, and horses. Families and their animals lived under the same roof, with the animals at one end of the house and the people at the other. In general, the houses were about 45 feet long and 15 feet wide, with thatched roofs. For warmth and cooking, people burned dried peat, with the smoke going out a hole in the roof. Sparks from the burning peat often set fire to the roofs. In the ruins of burned houses archeologists have found many clues to how the people lived.

Still other clues have come from graves. In the early part of the Iron Age, the dead were burned on funeral pyres. The bones of a dead person were later placed in an urn and buried, sometimes surrounded by a circle of stones. The dead seem to have had little in the way of grave goods. Archeologists have found only a few pieces of jewelry—brooches and iron pins—iron shears and razors, and belt buckles.

Later, funeral customs changed in some parts of Denmark. The dead were buried in graves, where they were placed on

A number of Iron Age houses have been built in modern times, based on the findings of archeologists.

their sides in a sleeping position. With them were many kinds of grave goods. The richest graves held beautiful sets of drinking cups and large containers made of finely worked bronze, silver, and glass, all from Rome.

The Iron Age people worshiped various gods. Like even earlier peoples, they believed that the peat bogs were the dwelling places of the gods. And there they made offerings to the gods. Peasants put steaks, legs of meat, or porridge in pottery containers and placed these in the bogs. Thousands

The Gundestrup Cauldron,
a large silver container,
was one of the bog offerings
to the gods. Scenes on the
Cauldron show gods and
their attendants, mythical
animals, and a human
sacrifice (see details below).

of such containers have been found, with ancient offerings meant to ensure a good harvest or to thank the gods for their help. Warriors broke the weapons of a defeated enemy and placed them in the bog to thank the gods for victory. Priests and chieftains placed great treasures, such as bronze and silver containers, in the bogs as offerings to the gods.

The bog offerings raise a question: Were the bog people also being offered to the gods? Is that why they were killed and placed in the bogs?

The Iron Age people of Denmark did not normally bury their dead in bogs. The funeral pyres and graves make that clear. It is possible that some of the bog people died by accident—that they may have walked in dangerous areas and sunk into the bogs. It is possible that some of them were murdered and their bodies hidden in the bogs. But most seem to have been killed elsewhere and then placed in a bog, often in a peat cutting. They seem in some way to have been special.

Two explanations can be found in the writings of the Roman historian Tacitus. One has to do with punishment. The other has to do with religious sacrifices, of which there are many examples in ancient times.

Whenever people live together in groups, they develop rules of behavior. The rules may have their roots in religious beliefs. They may be based on what is best for the community in general. People are expected to obey the rules. Those who break them are punished.

In writing about the northern tribes, Tacitus says that

traitors and deserters were hanged from trees. Cowards, poor fighters, and men of evil habits were plunged into the bogs and pinned down with branches. Women who sinned had their hair cut off and were driven out of the villages.

If Tacitus was correct, then some of the bog mummies must be the bodies of people who had been punished. Perhaps the Iron Age people believed that those who broke the rules had angered the gods. The punishment was death, and the bodies were peace offerings to the gods.

Tacitus also says that the northern tribes worshiped several gods, but the chief one was Mother Earth. They did not build temples to her but worshiped her in sacred groves, as their ancestors had. Once a year all the people who were related by blood sent delegates to a sacred grove. There they began their rites with a human sacrifice, made to Mother Earth for the good of the community.

So far, Tacitus' explanations are the best available. But there is not enough archeological evidence to prove that either or both are true. It is, for example, easy to believe that the Tollund and Grauballe men were sacrificed at the time of year when Mother Earth would again bring spring and cause seeds to sprout—the very kinds of seeds that had gone into each last meal. It is equally easy to believe that they ate a typical winter meal and were put to death as punishment for some crime; quite by chance their bodies were placed in the bogs at a time of year when temperatures were ideal for preserving them.

The fuller tale that the bog mummies have to tell will not

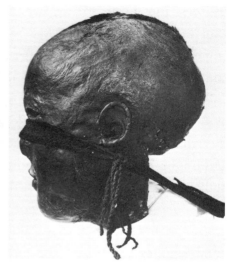

In 1948 peat cutters near Osterby in West Germany came upon the head of a man wrapped in a deerskin cape. His hair was about eleven inches long, parted at the back, and gathered on the right side of his head into a skillfully formed knot. Such hair knots are described by Tacitus, who says it was particularly men of the Swabian tribe who wore these knots.

The body of a girl, aged about fourteen, was found by peat cutters outside Schleswig, West Germany, in 1952. The hair had been shaved off the left side of her head and cropped short on the right. A brightly colored headband had apparently been used as a blindfold or a gag. The girl was naked except for the band and a fur collar. The body of a middle-aged man was found some fifteen feet away. He appeared to have been choked to death with a hazel stick that lay around his neck. Both bodies date from the same period, but there is no way of telling whether they were put in the bog at the same time.

be known until more of them have been thoroughly examined. Of the many that have been found, only some have been preserved. Of these, only a few have been studied. A few samples cannot yield the kind of patterns that scientists look for. One important unanswered question, for instance, has to do with the different ways people were put to death and placed in bogs. Do the differences reflect the periods in which the people were killed, or do they reflect the reasons for putting them to death? Only the dating of many more bodies may answer that question. And so, like other mummies, the bog bodies still have many more tales to tell.

For Further Reading

For Further Reading

means especially suitable for young readers

*Aliki. *Mummies Made in Egypt.* New York: Thomas Y. Crowell, 1979.

Artamonov, M. I. "Frozen Tombs of the Scythians." *Scientific American*, May 1965.

Cockburn, Aidan and Eve, eds. *Mummies, Disease, and Ancient Cultures.* New York: Cambridge University Press, 1980.

*David, Rosalie, ed. *Mysteries of the Mummies.* New York: Charles Scribner's Sons, 1979.

*Glob, P. V. *The Bog People: Iron-Age Man Preserved.* Translated from the Danish by Rupert L. Bruce-Mitford. Ithaca, N.Y.: Cornell University Press, 1969.

*Harris, James E., and Kent R. Weeks. *X-raying the Pharaohs.* New York: Charles Scribner's Sons, 1973.

Leca, Ange-Pierre. *The Egyptian Way of Death: Mummies and the Cult of the Immortal.* Garden City, N.Y.: Doubleday & Company, Inc., 1981.

*McHargue, Georgess. *Mummies.* New York. J. B. Lippincott Company, 1972.

*Madison, Arnold. *Mummies in Fact and Fiction.* New York: Franklin Watts, Inc., 1980.

*Pace, Mildred Mastin. *Wrapped for Eternity: The Story of the Egyptian Mummy.* New York: McGraw-Hill, Inc., 1974.

Index

Index

parasites (*continued*)
    hookworm in Americas, 74
    in Egypt, 43, 46
    in mummy 1770, 52, 54, 59
peat cuttings, 85
peat moss, 82, 84
Peru, 18
    see also Ica, Inca Empire, Pisco
    Valley
Pisco Valley
    cemetery, 76
    Indian-Spanish contact, 76–79
    Indian miners, 77–79
    injuries, 77–79

Rameses III, *31*
Rameses V, *46*
resin, 29, 32
Romans
    and Iron Age peoples, 93, 97
    rule in Egypt, *33*, 57

St. Lawrence Island, 13
Scythians
    clothing, *14*
    embalming, 16
    funeral customs, 16–18
    horses, 14, 17
    way of life, 14
Seti I, *31*
Sicily (Palermo), 10
Spanish conquest, *62*, 63–66,
    69–72, 76–79

sphagnum, 82, 84

Tacitus, 100–101, *102*
Tashat, Lady, *45*
teeth
    as clues to age, 58–59
    of Egyptians, 46–48
    of Peruvian coastal dwellers, 74,
        76
Thutmosis I, *41*
Thutmosis IV, *40*
Tiye, Queen, *43*
Tollund man
    cause of death, 82, *83*
    clothing, 82, *83*
    described, 81–82, 85
    discovery of, 81
    head, *80*
    how different, 87
    last meal, 85
tsantsas, 18–20
Tutankhamen, *43*

Valley of the Kings, *43*

x-rays
    of animal mummies, *34–38*
    of bog bodies, 85, *88*
    of Egyptian mummies, *38*, 40–49,
        51–52
    used to study mummies, 39–42,
        46–48, 51–54, 72

Photo Credits

Photo Credits